Turbulent Planet

Earth Erupts

Volcanoes

EXPRESS EDITION

Mary Colson

www.raintreepublishers.co.uk
Visit our website to find out more information about **Raintree** books.

To order:
☎ Phone 44 (0) 1865 888113
▤ Send a fax to 44 (0) 1865 314091
▢ Visit the Raintree Bookshop at **www.raintreepublishers.co.uk** to browse our catalogue and order online.

First published in Great Britain by Raintree Publishers,
Halley Court, Jordan Hill, Oxford , OX2 8EJ,
part of Harcourt Education Ltd.
Raintree is a registered trademark of Harcourt Education Ltd.

Produced for Raintree Publishers by Discovery Books Ltd.
Editorial: Andrew Farrow, Louise Galpine, Janine de Smet,
Charlotte Guillain, and Isabel Thomas
Design: Victoria Bevan and Ian Winton
Picture Research: Maria Joannou and Ginny Stroud-Lewis
Consultant: Keith Lye
Production: Duncan Gilbert and Jonathan Smith
Printed and bound in China by South China
Printing Company
Originated by Dot Gradations Ltd, UK

ISBN 1844437043 (hardback)
09 08 07 06 05
10 9 8 7 6 5 4 3 2 1

ISBN 1844437256 (paperback)
09 08 07 06 05
10 9 8 7 6 5 4 3 2 1

British Library Cataloguing in Publication Data
Colson, Mary
Earth erupts: volcanoes. – (Freestyle express. Turbulent
planet)
1. Volcanoes – Juvenile literature 2. Volcanic eruptions –
Juvenile literature
I. Title
551.2'1
A full catalogue record for this book is available from the
British Library.

This levelled text is a version of Freestyle: Turbulent planet:
Earth erupts.

Photo acknowledgements
p.4/5, FLPA/Dr. Guest; p.4, FLPA/S. Jonasson; p.5 bottom,
Corbis/Michael S. Yamashita; p.5 middle, Corbis/Bo
Zaunders; p.5 top, Photodisc; p.6/7, FLPA/Silvesiris
Fotoservice; p.6, PA Photos/EPA; p.7, Corbis/Michael S.
Yamashita; p.9, Corbis/Galen Rowell; p.10, Art Directors &
Trip; p.12/13, PA Photos/PANA-JIJ; p.12, Lonely
Planet/Brent Winebrenner; p.13, Corbis/J.D. Griggs; p.14/15,
Corbis/Galen Rowell; p.14, Corbis; p.15, FLPA; p.16,
Corbis/Bo Zaunders; p.17, Associated press/Michael Pobst;
p.18 left, Corbis/Bob Krist; p.18 right, Photodisc; p.19, PA
Photos/EPA; p.20, Getty Images/Imagebank; p.21,
NASA/NSSDC/GSFC; p.22 right, FLPA/R. Holcomb – USGS;
p.23, Oxford Scientific Films/T. C. Middleton; p.24/25,
FLPA/S. Jonasson; p.24, PA Photos/EPA; p.25, Corbis/
Bettman; p.26, Popperfoto; p.27 left, Oxford Scientific
Films/E. R. Degginger/AA; p.27 right, Science Photo
Library/Jeremy Bishop; p.28/29, Associated Press/Bullit
Marque; p.28, Corbis; p.29, Corbis/Charles O'Rear; p.30/31,
Corbis/Charles Mauzy; p.30, Oxford Scientific Films/James J.
Robinson; p.32/33, Corbis/Chloe Harford Sygma; p.32,
Corbis/Bettman; p.33, Associated Press/NOAA; p.34 bott,
Corbis/James A Sugar; p.34 top, Oxford Scientific Films/
Ronald Toms; p.35, Oxford Scientific Films/Mary Plage;
p.36/37, PA Photos/EPA; p.36, Associated Press/Stringer;
p.37, FLPA/MarkNewman; p.38 left, Corbis/Bossu Regis;
p.38 right, Reuters Picture Archive/Jacky Naegelen; p.39, Jeff
Schmaltz, MODIS Rapid Response Team, NASA GSFC;
p.40/41, Corbis/Roger Ressmeyer; p.40, FLPA/S. Jonasson;
p.42/43, FLPA/G. Prola, Panda Photo; p.42, PA Photos/EPA;
p.43, Corbis/Roger Ressmeyer; p.44, Corbis/Galen Rowell;
p.45, Corbis/Bettman

Cover photograph reproduced with permission of NHPA/
Kevin Schafer

Disclaimer
All the Internet addresses (URLs) given in this book were valid
at the time of going to press. However, due to the dynamic
nature of the Internet, some addresses may have changed, or
sites may have changed or ceased to exist since publication.
While the author and Publishers regret any inconvenience this
may cause readers, no responsibility for any such changes can
be accepted by either the author or the Publishers.

Contents

Any words appearing in the text in bold, **like this**, are explained in the glossary. You can also look out for some of them in the Hot words box at the bottom of each page.

Fire mountain

Without warning

There are about 500 volcanoes around the world that could erupt at any time, like the one below. No one can predict how violent the **eruption** will be.

Deep below the surface of the Earth, super-hot liquid rock and gases are bubbling and boiling. Huge **pressure** is building up. **Molten** rock is being forced up to the surface.

Blow up!

Suddenly, fiery ashes and rock are hurled through an opening in a mountain top. The molten rock glows golden-orange. Spitting fire explodes in the air. Smoke bellows out. A stream of hot liquid rock called **lava** flows down. The lava covers everything in its path.

Hot words   molten   melted

Deadly power

Clouds of hot gases and ash pour out. They rush downhill at over 300 kilometres (185 miles) per hour. The air is thick with falling ash and rocks. Lightning cracks overhead. The sounds are deafening.

Rivers of lava stream down. The lava sets fire to crops and forests. People run for their lives. It is a terrifying experience. But it is also spectacular and exciting. This is a volcano **erupting**.

Scientists study volcanoes to learn more about their activity. This is Mount Kilauea in the Hawaiian Islands.
▽

Find out later . . .

. . . how volcanic eruptions change the weather.

. . . why this castle is built on an old volcano.

. . . what ancient people believed about volcanoes.

erupt   when a volcano throws out gas, fire, and ash

Amazing magma

Magma is molten rock and gas that lies deep underground. When magma is forced out of the Earth's surface through a volcano, it is called lava.

God of fire

For centuries people have tried to explain the power of volcanoes. Some believed that volcanoes were the work of angry gods and goddesses.

The Romans were the first to use the name 'volcano'. It comes from the name Vulcan, their god of fire. The Romans believed Vulcan was a blacksmith. They thought that the rumblings of mountains came from his forge underground.

A river of lava flows down the slopes of Mount Etna in Sicily, Italy, towards the island of Zafferana.

△ Lava from Mount Kilauea in the Hawaiian Islands flows constantly into the sea.

magma   very hot liquid rock and gases

Volcano beliefs

There was a Roman **myth** that a 100-headed monster called Typhon was buried under Mount Etna in Sicily. The volcano **erupted** when Typhon was trying to escape.

Islanders in Samoa believe that a god is shaking their island in anger when there is an **eruption**.

Some Caribbean people used to pray to volcano gods to protect their land from evil.

Hawaiian beliefs

Some Hawaiians believe that Pele, the goddess of fire, appears before an eruption. In this picture, a Hawaiian man is making an offering to Pele.

myth   ancient story that is usually untrue

What causes volcanoes?

To understand what causes volcanoes, we need to know how the Earth is made up.

There are three main parts.
- In the middle is the ultra-hot, solid, inner **core** and liquid, outer core
- Around this is the mainly solid **mantle**
- Near the top of the mantle are liquid rock and gases called **magma**
- On the outside is the **crust**, the surface of the Earth.

How a volcano erupts

Red-hot magma lies deep underground.

Where there are weaknesses in the crust, magma pushes to the surface.

▼

Near the surface the magma expands.

▼

Lava bursts out of the volcano.

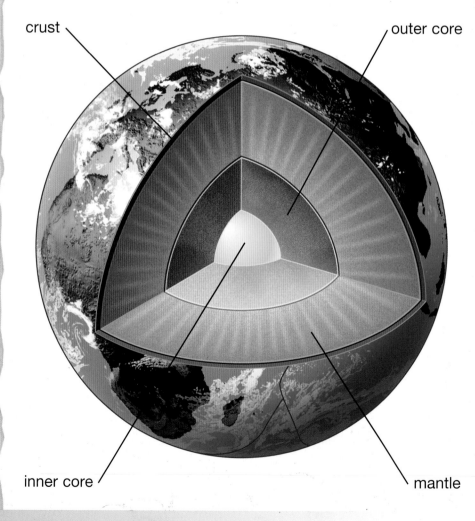

crust

outer core

inner core

mantle

How a volcano is formed

A volcano begins life as magma in the Earth's mantle about 100 kilometres (60 miles) below the surface.

When **pressure** builds up, the magma rises towards the surface. The magma is then forced upwards through a weaker part of the crust. The magma escapes through a hole called a **vent** in the Earth's surface.

The steep slopes of these volcanoes are built up of layers of ash and hardened lava. ▽

mantle   Earth's layer that lies between the core and the crust

Moving Earth

The Earth's **crust** is divided into enormous **plates,** or slabs, that are constantly moving.

Some plates have land on them. They are called **continental** plates. Others are under seas and oceans. They are called oceanic plates. Many plates are part continental, part oceanic.

Making mountains

Mountain ranges were formed millions of years ago by two continental plates meeting head-on. As they push upwards, their edges buckle. Thick layers of rock are folded into mountain chains.

The snow-capped ▷ Himalayas in Nepal and China are the highest mountain range in the world.

Hot words   continental   to do with one of the Earth's main land masses

Plate power

In some places, plates are pulling apart from each other. This creates great **tension** in the rocks. Sometimes, oceanic plates are pushing against each other. When this happens one plate may be pushed under another plate. Sometimes plates grind or slide past each other.

Most volcanoes are found near the edges of plates.

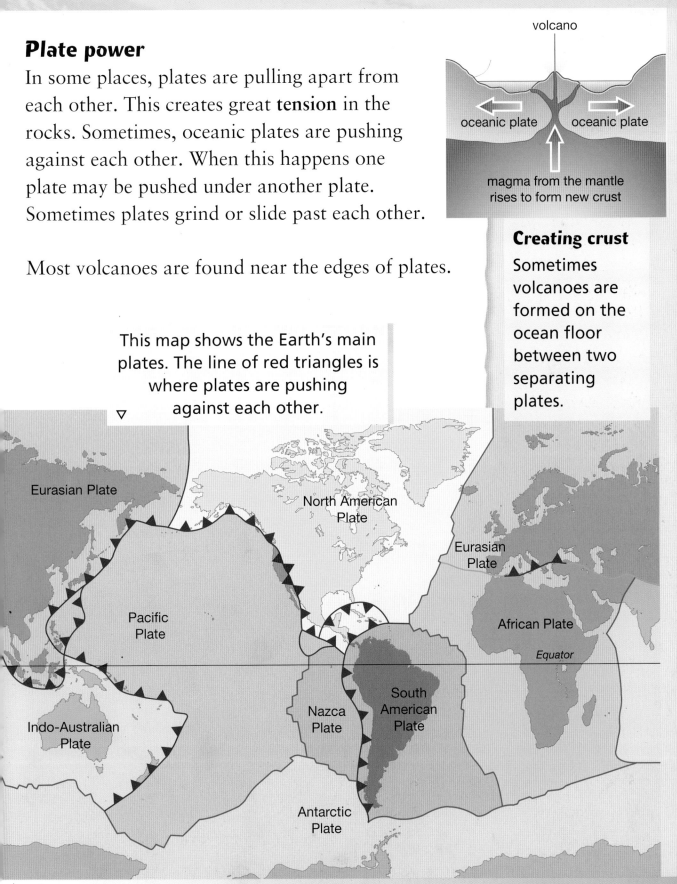

volcano

oceanic plate   oceanic plate

magma from the mantle rises to form new crust

Creating crust

Sometimes volcanoes are formed on the ocean floor between two separating plates.

This map shows the Earth's main plates. The line of red triangles is where plates are pushing against each other.

Eurasian Plate

North American Plate

Eurasian Plate

Pacific Plate

African Plate

Equator

Indo-Australian Plate

Nazca Plate

South American Plate

Antarctic Plate

plate   rigid sections of the Earth's hard outer layers

Active, dormant, or extinct

An **active volcano** is one that still **erupts**. Some volcanoes may be active almost all the time. Others can be fairly active and then become dormant. A **dormant volcano** has not erupted for a long time. This may be from a few years to several centuries. An **extinct volcano** has stopped erupting altogether.

Mount Fuji is a famous ▷ strato-volcano. It towers over the city of Shimizu in Japan.

Highest volcano

At 6887 metres (22,595 feet) high, Nevados Ojos del Salado in Chile (above) is the world's highest active volcano. It is eighteen times as high as the Empire State Building in New York City.

Strato-volcanoes

There are several types of volcano. Some erupt like an explosion. They hurl **lava** into the air. Others are quieter and produce runny lava.

Strato-volcanoes erupt in both ways. These volcanoes are cone-shaped. They are made up of layers of ash and hardened lava. See the photo below.

△   These scientists at Kilauea, Hawaii, are collecting lava. This is dangerous work in burning hot temperatures.

Looking and learning

Scientists study rock and lava to learn more about volcanoes. They try to predict how violent a volcano's next **eruption** will be.

extinct volcano   volcano that has stopped erupting

Mauna Kea

Mauna Kea, in Hawaii, is a **dormant** shield **volcano**. It has not erupted for about 3500 years. It has gentle slopes and a flat **summit**.

Shield volcanoes

Shield **volcanoes** are flatter and lower than **strato-volcanoes**. The **lava** flows fast. It does not have time to cool and form into a cone. Mauna Loa and Kilauea in Hawaii are shield volcanoes. They have frequent and powerful **eruptions**.

Ngorongoro Crater in Tanzania is home to animals like elephants, buffaloes, zebras, and wildebeest. Also, there are over one hundred species of birds.
▽

summit   highest point of a mountain

Caldera volcanoes

When a volcano **erupts**, the force of the explosion can destroy the top of the cone. It then collapses inwards. A huge basin called a **caldera** is formed. This can occur on both strato- and shield volcanoes. The world's largest caldera is Ngorongoro Crater in Tanzania.

Stromboli island

The lava from this volcanic island near Sicily, Italy, flows continuously into the sea. The eruptions are spectacular but dangerous.

caldera   large, basin-shaped crater

Movers and shakers

About 75 per cent of the world's volcanoes occur in one area of the Pacific Ocean. This area is called the Ring of Fire. See the map below. Some of the Earth's largest volcanic **eruptions** occur here.

Solid rock

Edinburgh Castle in Scotland (above) is built on the remains of an **extinct volcano**. The castle was built there because it is high above the valley. It was therefore difficult to attack.

Hundreds of volcanoes can be found in the Ring of Fire which ▽ circles the Pacific Ocean.

Eurasian Plate

North American Plate

Mount St Helens ▲

Mount Fuji ▲

Paricutin ▲

Arenal ▲

Mount Pinatubo ▲

Pacific Plate

Cotopaxi ▲

Rabaul ▲

Krakatau ▲ Tambora

Nazca Plate

South American Plate

Indo-Australian Plate

Cerro Azul ▲

Antarctic Plate

Key to map
▲ famous volcano
— Ring of Fire
— plate boundary

▲ Erebus

◁ Steam and lava escaping from fissures are a sign of Iceland's volcanic activity.

The VEI

Scientists can measure the power of eruptions using the Volcanic Explosivity Index or VEI. The index goes from 0 to 8. It can measure the height of the eruption cloud. It can also record how long the eruption lasts.

Fissures

Sometimes, a crack may open up in the ground in volcanic regions. It may tear open into a **fissure** many kilometres long. Great amounts of hot gases and **lava** are released.

Iceland has a lot of volcanoes with many fissures running across the land. The lava is very fluid. It may spread out to cover a large area.

fissure long, thin crack in rock from which lava and gases escape

Pinatubo's power

In 1991, after some small explosions, Mount Pinatubo in the Philippines **erupted** violently. It had not erupted for 600 years. A huge amount of ash and rock was **ejected** from the volcano. The ash and rock was almost 200 metres (656 feet) thick in places.

Hard to believe

Outside the Mirage Hotel in Las Vegas, USA, crowds gather every evening to watch a spectacular artificial volcano. A tranquil waterfall by day, it 'erupts' into flames at night.

The gigantic ash ▷ cloud from Pinatubo's eruption rose 35 kilometres (22 miles) into the air.

Hot words   eject   send, or drive out, by force

Disaster area

Mount Pinatubo's **eruption** was one of the largest of the 20th century. Many people lost their homes. About 800 people died.

Mount Nyiragongo

In 2002, in the African Republic of Congo, Mount Nyiragongo erupted. The **lava** from this volcano destroyed twelve villages. Many people had to **evacuate** their homes.

Goma

A hotel signboard is all that remains in this part of Goma (below) after lava from Mount Nyiragongo in Africa rushed through the city.

Underwater volcanoes

Underwater volcanoes are called **seamounts**. When a seamount **erupts** a few extra large waves appear on the surface of the sea. All **eruptions** release gas into the sea. Sometimes, the gas is poisonous and can kill fish.

The diagram shows a seamount, trench, and spreading ridge. ▽

Undersea activity

Many of the world's **active volcanoes** are seamounts. In the picture above, divers are examining the **vent** of a seamount in the Pacific Ocean.

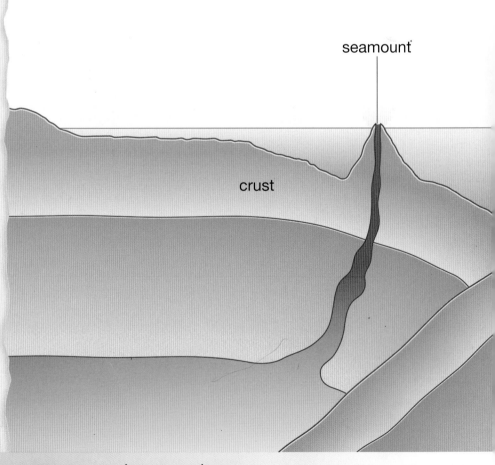

seamount

crust

Trenches

Long, deep **trenches** form under the sea when two **plates collide**. One plate is forced under the other. This causes **magma** to rise to the surface. The huge **stress** of the plates moving may cause a volcanic eruption.

Ridges

An oceanic ridge is a long range of underwater mountains. It forms between plates that are moving apart. Magma is forced between the plates. It then hardens to form new rock. As new magma keeps pushing up, the ridge grows and widens.

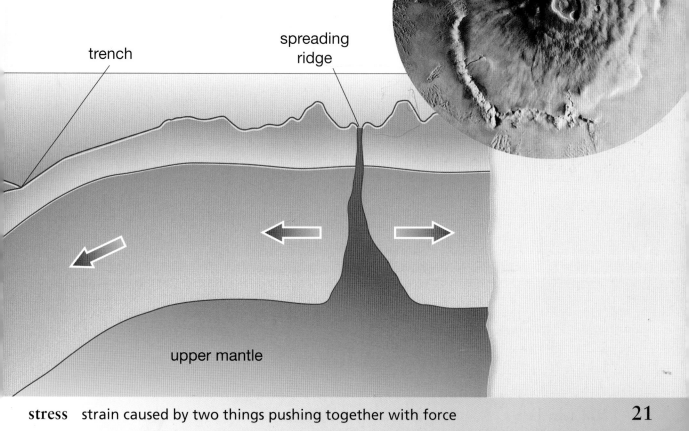

trench

spreading ridge

upper mantle

---

stress   strain caused by two things pushing together with force

Measuring volcanoes

We can sometimes predict when a volcano will **erupt**. **Vulcanologists** study volcanoes to learn more about their activity, and to predict any eruptions in the future.

Dangerous job
Vulcanologists work in **hazardous** conditions. This heat suit (above) protects the vulcanologist from the heat of **lava** up to 1150 °C (2102 °F).

△ This vulcanologist is studying hardened lava.

vulcanologist   scientist who studies volcanoes

Recording change

Teams of vulcanologists usually work together on a volcano for safety reasons. Some of their work is done safely indoors. Some of their work is set up close to **active volcanoes**. Vulcanologists use different ways to record these changes.

Working together

Vulcanologists work with **geologists**, who study rocks and **plate** movements. They also work with seismologists, who study earthquakes. These experts piece together as much information as possible about a volcano.

Tiltmeter

The surface of a volcano changes shape when **magma** moves or rises from below. Vulcanologists use different ways to **monitor** these changes. One of their instruments is called a **tiltmeter**. It measures very small shifts in the surface of a volcano before and during an eruption.

Difficult climb
This vulcanologist is being lowered on a safety wire into a hole in the lava.

geologist   scientist who studies rocks

Staying put
Even when an eruption is predicted, some people refuse to leave their homes. They want to stay to protect their property and **livelihoods**.

Fertile farmland

It may seem risky, but millions of people choose to live close to a volcano. They want to take advantage of the **fertile** soil.

Added nutrients

After an **eruption**, the farmland is coated in volcanic ash. This adds **nutrients** to the soil. Nutrients are chemicals that help plants to grow well.

In some countries, it is possible to start planting crops within two years of an eruption.

Surtsey island

In Iceland, in 1963, a new island rose above sea level during a fiery underwater eruption. Afterwards, ash rained down over a wide area.

New plants

When the new island cooled, scientists discovered the soil was very fertile. Eventually, over 50 different plants started to grow there.

Lava flow

Orange-red and scorching hot, this **lava** flow is fast and furious. As it cools, it turns into rock with a smooth, rippled surface.

◁ New plant life begins to grow only a few months after an eruption in Iceland.

Eruption!

Did you know...?

- Mount Erebus was discovered in 1841 by British explorers.

- In 1979 a sight-seeing plane from New Zealand crashed into its **summit**. All 257 people on board were killed.

Antarctica is the world's coldest **continent**. Even in this freezing climate, volcanoes are found throughout the region. Some of these **volcanoes** are **active**. Beautiful, snow-capped Mount Erebus has been **erupting** for years in the middle of all the ice.

Volcanoes in the Antarctic do not melt the ice because there is so much of it. ▷

Mount Etna

Mount Etna, on the island of Sicily in Italy, has been active for thousands of years. It has erupted many times. In October 2002, after more than 100 **tremors**, it erupted again. The **lava** flowed dangerously close to two towns. People had to be **evacuated**.

The glowing **magma** shooting out of Mount Etna, Italy, can look like a huge firework display. ▽

Friendly giant?

Mount Etna is Europe's largest active volcano. Its nickname is the 'friendly giant'. This is because only 73 recorded deaths have been caused by **eruptions** in its whole history.

Cracking Krakatau

One of the loudest and most violent **eruptions** was on a tropical island in Indonesia in 1883. The island was called Krakatau.

The island was at the base of an old volcano. The volcano had not **erupted** for 200 years.

The eruption blasted away almost the whole island.

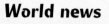

The volcano on the new island of Anak Krakatau continues to erupt and grow. ▽

pumice   light volcanic rock

Blowing its top

The eruption shot **pumice** and ash clouds 35 kilometres (22 miles) into the air.

The volcano's sides collapsed into the sea. This created a huge wave called a **tsunami**. The tsunami was nearly 40 metres (131 feet) high.

The tsunami destroyed villages on nearby islands. More than 36,000 people drowned.

New island

In 1927, volcanic eruptions on the seafloor started to form a new island exactly where Krakatau had been. The new island is called Anak Krakatau, which means 'Child of Krakatau'.

tsunami   huge wave caused by earthquakes, volcanic eruptions, or landslides

Enormous eruptions

In 1980, a powerful **eruption** occurred in the Cascade Mountains in the north-west of the USA. A volcano called Mount St Helens was struck by an earthquake deep underground.

The earthquake caused a mighty volcanic eruption. The eruption blew a **crater** nearly 2 kilometres (1.2 miles) wide in the **summit**.

Mount St Helens

Ten million trees were flattened in the eruption of Mount St Helens (above).

crater   opening at the top of a volcano

Supervolcanoes

Supervolcanoes are volcanoes that produce the largest eruptions in the world. A supervolcano lies underneath the Yellowstone National Park in the central Rocky Mountains of the USA. See the photo below.

The supervolcano last **erupted** over 600,000 years ago. **Vulcanologists** now think it may erupt again.

If the supervolcano under Yellowstone National Park (below) erupted, it could be thousands of times bigger than the blast at Mount St Helens.

▽

Hot spots

Some volcanoes, like the Yellowstone supervolcano and those on Hawaii, lie far from **plate** edges. They lie over **hot spots** in the top of the **mantle**.

hot spot   area of great heat

Mount Soufrière, Montserrat

In 1995, a small **eruption** occurred on the Caribbean island of Montserrat. A **dormant volcano** called Mount Soufrière burst into life.

A second huge explosion in 1997 caused massive destruction. Then in 1998, the volcano **erupted** without warning. Today, most of Montserrat is still a danger zone.

Instant danger

Erupting volcanoes can have dramatic effects on the weather. Lightning strikes, as shown below, are common.

La Palma, Canary Islands

Scientists believe that a huge part of the island of La Palma, in the Canary Islands, could fall into the sea. This might happen next time the island's volcano erupts.

The power of the rock **landslide** would cause a giant **tsunami**. The wave would be over 500 metres (1640 feet) high.

Terrifying tsunamis

Tsunamis cannot be seen while they are building up out at sea. The machine (below) detects tsunamis before they hit the shoreline. This allows scientists to give early warnings.

◁ After Montserrat's 1998 eruption, a layer of grey ash covered the town of Plymouth on the island.

landslide　downward movement of land that can carry whole hillsides away

Types of eruption

Some volcanoes hurl out masses of gases, ash, and lumps of **molten** rock. They do not produce **lava**. Others produce fast-flowing lava but do not explode violently. Three main types of **eruption** are described here.

Hawaiian

The lava in a Hawaiian eruption is very runny. It travels fast and may cover a large area. The lava builds up into a **shield volcano**. Little volcanic ash is formed. This is called the 'quiet' type of eruption. Kilauea on Hawaii **erupts** in this way.

Did you know …?

The Hawaiians have special words to describe hardened lava. Pahoehoe (pronounced 'pa-ho-ee-ho-ee') sets into smooth, gentle folds and rolls. It looks like twisted rope.

◁ This Hawaiian eruption is producing thin, runny lava. This forms shield volcanoes.

shield volcano   low, dome-shaped volcano

Strombolian

In a Strombolian eruption, the lava is less runny than in a Hawaiian eruption. It does not flow as easily or as far. Small lumps of lava spurt from the **crater**. Smoke and ash is also thrown out. Strombolian eruptions are named after the volcanic island of Stromboli in Italy.

Plinian

This is the most violent and destructive eruption of all. Hot, thick lava **fragments**, huge clouds of very hot ash, and gases rush down the volcano's sides. Mount Etna, Europe's largest volcano, has Plinian eruptions.

Pliny the Elder

Plinian eruptions are named after the Roman writer, Pliny the Elder. He was killed by the eruption of Vesuvius, the Italian volcano, in AD 79.

◁ These deadly clouds are from a Plinian eruption of the Mayon volcano in the Philippines.

fragments small bits and pieces

After-effects

Hunger

Clouds of volcanic ash, like those shown below, can destroy crops. This may lead to food shortages and a risk of **famine**.

If you live near an **active volcano**, you should prepare an emergency plan:

- Work out two escape routes from each room in your home
- Learn how to turn off power supplies
- Write a list of emergency telephone numbers
- Pick two meeting places in case your family is separated.

When the volcano **erupts**, you need to act fast. Follow the checklist below:

Survival Checklist

- Listen to the radio for warnings.
- Be prepared to leave your home quickly.
- Do not try to pack all your belongings.
- Make sure all your family get out of the house.
- Cover your mouth and nose to prevent breathing in ash. Wear goggles to protect your eyes.
- Go to the nearest evacuation point – quickly.

Hot words   famine extreme lack of food

After an eruption

Volcanic **eruptions** can **pollute** drinking water and spread disease. Gas, electricity, and water may be cut off. Road and rail links may be destroyed.

The **emergency services** and air and land rescue teams must be ready to respond. Medical teams and even the army are called in to help. Charity and aid agencies are ready to deliver food and medicines.

About 30,000 tourists used to visit Stromboli (below) in Italy each year. In 2002, tourists were banned because the volcano had become too dangerous.

Disaster Prevention Day in Japan is 1 September each year. Emergency **drills** are held in schools and ▽ offices around the country.

emergency services   police, ambulance, and fire brigade

Climate change

After the 1991 **eruption** of Mount Pinatubo in the Philippines, world temperatures fell by about 0.5 °C (0.9 °F). Poisonous gases from the eruption upset the Earth's **atmosphere**.

Scientists believe that Pinatubo caused a drop in temperatures for a few years afterwards. Harvests failed because of the colder weather and the air **pollution**.

Refugees who have fled from a volcanic eruption are waiting for food supplies. ▽

Acid rain

As a volcano **erupts**, it spits out gases into the Earth's atmosphere. They mix with water vapour to form **acid** rain. When strong acid rain falls it can destroy whole forests.

Hot words   acid   substance that can eat away solids or damage plants

Rock uses

Volcanoes are very destructive but they do have some benefits. Some of the rocks from volcanoes are very useful. For example, **pumice** is a light rock formed from **lava**. It is used for grinding and polishing stones and metals. It can also be used in your bathtub for scrubbing hard skin.

Another type of **volcanic rock** is used for building roads. It is very hard-wearing.

The eruption of Mount Etna on Sicily can be seen from space. ▽

Weird weather

The volcanic ash blasted into the atmosphere can block out sunlight for many months. After Krakatau erupted, the ash was carried around the world. It caused spectacular red sunsets.

refugee person forced to leave their area to escape war or natural disaster

39

Vesuvius, Italy, AD 79

A volcano called Mount Vesuvius **erupted** in Italy nearly 2000 years ago. The **eruption** happened near a city called Pompeii.

Violent eruption

Stones and ash from the violent eruption covered the city. Many people did not have time to escape. Many people died. The city was completely destroyed.

A plaster cast of one of the people who died in the eruption of Vesuvius. ▷

Iceland ash

These houses in Iceland (above) are surrounded by heaps of black ash after an eruption. It gives some idea of what happened during the Pompeii tragedy.

Uncovering the past

For nearly 1700 years, Pompeii lay completely undisturbed. When the city was uncovered, many buildings had been protected.

Human moulds

Ash had hardened around the bodies of humans to form **moulds**. The moulds remained, even though the bodies had decayed. Scientists poured liquid plaster into the moulds. When the plaster set, the moulds were chipped away. The shapes of the bodies could be seen at the moment of death.

At the ready

Scientists think that Vesuvius may erupt again soon. The Italian government has had **evacuation** and emergency plans in place for a few years, just in case.

mould   shaped hollow

The future

We cannot prevent volcanoes from **erupting**. But we can hope that developments in technology will help **vulcanologists** understand more about volcanoes. Today, some vulcanologists are studying the signals from **satellites**. This helps them to measure **plate** movements. Others use **laser beams** to detect changes underneath the surface of a volcano.

Hot water

Wild Japanese monkeys play in natural hot springs. These are heated by hot rocks deep beneath the Earth's surface.

Hot words   satellite   device orbiting the Earth that has been sent up into
space by a rocket

Dangers remain

Any of the world's 500 **active volcanoes** could erupt at any time. Even now, predicting **eruptions** is difficult and dangerous. There is still much to learn. One thing is clear, though. Volcanic eruptions remain one of the most thrilling and spectacular experiences of the natural world.

The cloud of gases rising from Mount Etna reminds us that a major eruption could occur soon. ▽

Staying safe

Thousands of people live and work in the shadow of active volcanoes. As scientists learn to predict eruptions more accurately, future disasters may be prevented.

laser beam   intense, artificial beam of light

Find out more

Websites

NASA Earth Observatory

Satellite pictures of volcanic eruptions from around the world, and more.
www.earthobservatory. nasa.gov/ NaturalHazards

Global Volcanism Program

Search for volcanic activity and data worldwide, plus weekly reports.
www.volcano.si.edu

BBC Science & Nature

News, features, and activities on natural disasters.
www.bbc.co.uk/sn/

Books

Disasters in Nature: Volcanoes,
    Catherine Chambers (Heinemann Library, 2001)
Excavating the Past: Ancient Rome,
    Fiona Macdonald (Heinemann Library, 2004)
Nature on the Rampage: Volcanoes,
    Christy Steele (Raintree, 2003)

World Wide Web

To find out more about volcanoes you can search the Internet. Use keywords like these:

- volcano +[country]
- "Ring of Fire"
- "shield volcano" +eruption

You can find your own keywords by using words from this book. The search tips opposite will help you find useful websites.

Search tips

There are billions of pages on the Internet. It can be difficult to find exactly what you are looking for. These tips will help you find useful websites more quickly:

- know what you want to find out
- use simple keywords
- use two to six keywords in a search
- only use names of people, places, or things
- put double quote marks around words that go together, for example "Ring of Fire"

Where to look

Search engine

A search engine looks through millions of website pages. It lists all the sites that match the words in the search box. You will find the best matches are at the top of the list, on the first page.

Search directory

A person instead of a computer has sorted a search directory. You can search by keyword or subject and browse through the different sites. It is like looking through books on a library shelf.

Glossary

acid   substance that can eat away solids or damage plants

active volcano   volcano that erupts constantly or occasionally

atmosphere   layer of air around the Earth

caldera   large, basin-shaped crater

collide   push against each other

continent   one of the Earth's main land masses

continental   to do with one of the Earth's main land masses

core   ultra-hot centre of the Earth

crater   opening at the top of a volcano

crust   outer, solid surface of the Earth

dormant volcano   volcano that has not erupted for a long time

drill   practice

eject   sent, or driven out, by force

emergency services   police, ambulance, and fire brigade

erupt   when a volcano throws out gas, fire, and ash

eruption   sudden force of gas, fire, and ash through the Earth's crust

evacuate   leave a place of danger

extinct volcano   volcano that has stopped erupting

famine   extreme lack of food

fertile   grows plants well

fissure   long, thin crack in rock from which lava and gases escape

forge   blacksmith's workshop

fragments   small bits and pieces

geologist   scientist who studies rocks

hazardous   dangerous

hot spot   area of great heat

landslide   downward movement of land that can carry whole hillsides away

laser beam   intense, artificial beam of light

lava   hot, melted rock that pours from a volcano

livelihood   how someone earns money to live on

magma   very hot liquid rock and gases

mantle   Earth's layer that lies between the core and the crust

molten   melted

monitor   watch closely

mould   shaped hollow

myth   ancient story that is usually untrue

nutrients   chemicals which help plants to grow

plate   rigid sections of the Earth's hard outer layers

pollute   add harmful substances to air, water, or land

pollution   harmful substances in the air, water, or land

pressure pushing force

pumice light volcanic rock

refugee person forced to leave their area to escape war or natural disaster

satellite device orbiting the Earth that has been sent up into space by a rocket

seamount underwater volcano

seismologist scientist who studies earthquakes

shield volcano low, dome-shaped volcano

strato-volcano steep-sided, cone-shaped volcano

stress strain caused by two things pushing together with force

summit highest point of a mountain

supervolcano volcano that produces the largest eruptions

tension pulling force

tiltmeter instrument that measures changes in a volcano's shape

tremor small earthquake

trench long, deep ditch or groove

tsunami huge wave caused by earthquakes, volcanic eruptions, or landslides

vent hole in the Earth's crust through which magma is forced out

volcanic rock rock formed from lava

vulcanologist scientist who studies volcanoes

Index